poems

These Moments of Arrest

sheila rosen

Big Tree Publishing
Langley, BC

Published by Big Tree Publishing
Surrey, BC Canada
ISBN: 978-1-9992463-3-4

bigtreepublishing.com

Designed by *Alexandrah Pahl*

For the
many
artists,
musicians,
poets
whom I've
quoted,
referenced,
been
inspired by.

THESE

Moments

of

ARREST

i   as when
people go
up with
flutes

ii in light
and colour
and form

Table of Contents

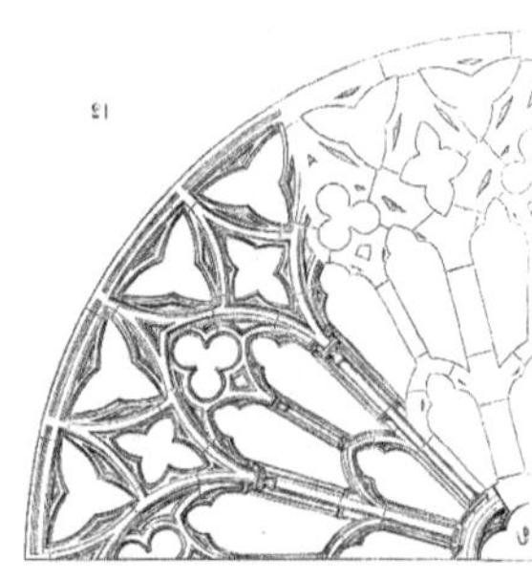

light and colour and form

Preface

Dear Reader,

These Poems were written over
a number of years as part of my
conversation with art and music
and our ever-fascinating world.
Some are directly ekphrastic, i.e.
describing or responding to a par-
ticular work of art. Many are more
general, reflecting times when I was
'arrested' by beauty or complexity
or simplicity in the world around
me. My hope is that some of my
poems will *'take you under arrest'*
and that in your reading and and in
your living, you will have moments
when *'something beautiful'* will pass
by your window, times when you
might experience *"a rendezvous of
the human psyche with 'otherness'"*
(George Steiner). Or to quote
Thomas Merton, moments when
*"art enables us to find ourselves and
lose ourselves at the same time."*

Sheila Rosen

Aspen Green, Vancouver BC
October, 2025

As
when
people
go
up.....

with flutes

Isaiah spoke of flutes
and the mountain of the Lord.
Shall we go up then? – not knowing
if the Lord is to be found
there, or in the valley, or on the way. Somewhere,
or everywhere (I've heard) He broods over waters,
inhabits hills and plains, seeks the health of nations.
Long ago He sent a poet blazing;
"your hearts will rejoice" said Isaiah
as when people go up with flutes."

Shall we give way then to Isaiah's confidence
in the willingness of our hearts to be made glad –
and go up with flutes?

Sting

Driving west into the sun — how jealously
it clings to the summer sky. In the CD player,
a burnished Best of Sting. His fields of gold
still breaking the heart. A song made to last.

Along Forty-ninth Ave., the people are out.
It's that kind of evening. Walking, jogging,
all on their legs, their same toddler legs
still holding. Made to last.

Stunning backlit world, your molecules
move like wind through fields of grass,
jarring every sense. Surely you are made
from everlasting to everlasting.

And you, weakling death, how you skulk
and run for cover on an evening
such as this. All the lovers laugh at you,
and all the children run

among the fields of barley.

Granddaughters Dancing 1 *(for Tadia, Kezia, Bethany)*

All your young lives, you've been gathering,
folding the world into yourselves,
winding it into enigmatic
balls of string.

Now you begin to unwind
the enigma, dancing yourselves
into the world. You are story-writing
on the stage floor in a moving, mutable script.

Granddaughters Dancing 2

Maggie's the one who danced in the aisle
of the Baptist Church at her Grandpa's funeral.
She was four and only knew how
to be Maggie.

Jaylene's the one who breaks
into random dances for big or small occasions —
it's called joie de vivre, being indomitable,
being Jaylene.

'Til we come round right.

"When true simplicity is gained
To bow and to bend we shan't be ashamed,
To turn, turn will be our delight,
'Til by turning, turning we come round right."
Simple Gifts - Shaker Hymn

Art is faint memory of a god, of God, if not God,
at least some grand hall wherein we danced in true
simplicity, waltzing without having to count one,
two, three, always coming round right, all steps
since that time, one long labyrinth of returning.

Was it a Mediterranean plaza where we were lucky
Greeks, arms entwined in a line, the bouzouki's plucked
strings throbbing, the rhythms accelerating. Or Cana
at Galilee and we the astonished Hebrews having a ball
with a hundred and fifty gallons of new best wine straight
from the vintner, saved for the last, never running dry.

A dim collective remembrance we can't seem to
shake. An imprinted impressionist piece, fading
often, to black, overlays of centuries, millennia; still
a grain of recall: our genesis, our original music
and the body's response: Art calling out to Eden.

Marimba

In the smallest house on the block someone
plays the marimba like a brook murmuring
burbling into the street. Picture the marimba
stretching from corner to corner, filling
the living room of the smallest house.

I knock on the door and ask,
"may I handle the marimba mallets?
run my hands over the keys? are they
real rosewood? do marimba makers'
hands smell of rosewood?" Marimba.

Marimba. The music loosens the memory net
and out shake the happy things of childhood:
a girl peddling her bicycle downhill,
her surrender to speed and the joy of that
surrender, not fearing. Not knowing
one day she'd hear a marimba and remember

the hill beside her house, the blue bicycle,
and in the living room, a marimba '78'
spinning fast on the turntable; remember
the timbre of the marimba, the nimbleness
of childhood, its limber surrender
to a kind of spinning joy.

Timpani

The timpani's bass boom
ending the symphony
is a boulder rolling toward
the stomach's pit, the heart's
pith, where a cauldron brews
its slurry of tears and elation.

A single percussive note breaks
through the hardpan which can crack
a shovel. I'm talking about my life,
its regrettable directions,
its plenitudes; that last lingering
boom of the timpani
seems to declare finality.
Or infinity. It threw me,
or I threw myself, under the rolling boulder.

Saxophone

You slide in under the sash
of my night-darkened window,
brash unholy instrument
breathing into my ear.

Crescendo, your midnight
wail pierces my skin,
dislodges the patch of ice
from underneath my breastbone.

Melt-water,
laden with leached salt
from new and ancient wounds,
spills over my cheekbones.

Now diminuendo you drizzle
your melody like warm butter
over trembling shoulders.
Ointment of release.

"Music was my refuge. I could crawl into
the space between the notes and curl my
back to loneliness."

Maya Angelou

Listening to Arvo Pärt in January

"It takes a great deal of strength to keep January out of the soul and I've failed this year." — *old Northridge in The Road Home by Jim Harrison*

Arvo, the Estonian, calls his music
white light - and you, a prism.
So his music, falling on your ears,
fractures light into infinite colours.

Or into its pain - if you go with Goethe
who said colour is the pain of light.
Inexplicably, what comes to mind
is a giant spruce splashing into understory.
Is such a falling refracted as colours of pain
only if someone hears? Does anybody hear?

Always, even with the lame word over which
you dilly-dallied, you hope poetry might arc across
to someone's thirsty circuitry.

Meantime parched and colourless, you want Arvo Pärt
to oust January from your soul. You want Arvo,
gentle insistent Estonian, to fall into you,
make of you a prism.

Bagatelle

Bach Beethoven Brahms, my childhood piano book.
And there, in ballpoint pen, my name in a child's best writing.
Leaf through frayed pages to Beethoven's Bagatelle No. 6
— what I perceive now as a small, skillfully cut gem.

Consider this Bagatelle, laid out before me, complete
in two pages (with noted repeats), awaiting skilled fingers,
simple though it is; awaiting the touch, the heart, to make
this jewel quietly shimmer in microcrystalline perfection.

Play it anyway, with my unpracticed, slightly arthritic hands.
Stay on the piano bench after partaking of the Bagatelle
and think on music, on poetry, how they aspire to
the inexpressible, the hidden, perhaps the unthinkable.

Admit to a desperate hunger of the poet inside me
to be done with my limping and stuttering; to write
instead, as near-perfect a jewel as Beethoven's Bagatelle;
to write (in some yet-to-be-found language) a shimmering.

Piano Speaks Her Mind

Place your hand on my frame and you'll know
potential energy awaiting conversion
into kinetic Mozart. Feel me brim and simmer,
strings quivering Scriabin even when
no hammer strikes. Something circles
inside me, a word, a memory. Name it.
The Brahms Intermezzo in A Major
you once brought to light, to life. Now
I remember what I am and why: a gift given
long ago for love. What is it comes
between us? Bring me your sweet fingers,
not fearing the smallness of your gift.

Tango

"Every time you take your partner in your arms, you improvise."
from a greeting card.

tango   is tradition plus improvisation
tango   is the ultimate intimate dance
tango   is an elegant pas de deux
tango   is glide pass embrace pause turn
tango   is a quick toss of the head, then together again
tango   is opening yourself to the rhythm of its music
tango   is opening yourself to the rhythm of your partner
tango   is feeling the music deep in your soul
tango   is tension and release
tango   is passion
tango   takes two

Aubade, Sunshine Coast

Morning, early,
on the sunshine coast
and a luthier is setting out
files, bits, clamps, cutters.

 He handles the living
sitka spruce, flamed maple
western red cedar, mahogany —
his wordless prayer of laying out.

The luthier's beloved quietly stirs
dark-roast winds in the studio kitchen,
lays white vessels on a blue cotton sea,
her prayer of laying out.

Beside the kitchen, her garden
raises its sleep-tousled head
the prolific results of spring's
prayer of laying out.

This is an aubade, a poem
appropriate to the dawn,
a prayer to be accompanied by
the music of quietude.

A prayer
for mahogany and maple
to one day flame into song.

Aubade, Thetis Island

He woke first and the sound
was, for a moment, no sound.

Yesterday they had wakened
to songbirds of many feathers
with the usual gulls and crows
to cause her annoyance.
But now, how strange
and rare — a caesura.

He began humming to fill in,
then one by one the birds joined him
and slowly she too came awake.
Last night, he had played his flute for her
sitting on the giant rock, while a seal
swam close. It had come just to listen
to music. That's what he told her.
She said there's probably good fishing.

She was dressing now and he played for her
"Dance me to the end of love,"
but she didn't seem to know it.
She's kind, he told himself,
and has a lovely way with water
when she swims. He said to her,
"Shall I compare thee to a summer's day?"

She looked puzzled, not knowing
what he might mean; nor did he
know where to go from there.
Then he began to know.
He would, of course,
see her home.

Ortlieb's

Late nights at Ortlieb's,
me, knowing the jazz standards -
only a bar from the band and I'd
name the song. "Nice one, Mom". Nice
to impress your kid for once. Philadelphia
was Philly and fun. Big, old, full of story,
philosophy, jazz. We were keen to listen.
To music and each other. This feast
moves into your past, moved by life's
events you don't see coming.
But for a short stretch of time,
it was pretty much pure jazz
and pure joy on dimly lit
North 3rd Street,
Philadelphia.

Quoting some Jazz Philosophers

“I merely took the energy it takes to pout
and wrote some blues.”

Duke Ellington

“Music is your own experience,
your thoughts, your wisdom. If you don’t live it,
it won’t come out your horn.”

Charlie Parker

“What we play is life.”

Louis Armstrong

Scat Song

Now that Ella's gone
I wanna say how it was –
small white girl, small town Canada
Lucky Lager Dance Time
and the Hit Parade bouncing
off the ionosphere into my room
in the dark of night. Then
a repeater station brought the CBC -
and I branched out, radio by daylight
and I remember Mona Lisa, Mona Lisa
men have named you. And Nature Boy,
a very strange enchanted boy and I
wanted to marry Nat King Cole.
I'd've said Yes just like that. I saw
Miss Ella Fitzgerald when I got to
the big city, old Georgia Auditorium,
me just a few feet from the stage.
Never got to see Nat Cole in real life.
Just as well, I guess, he was already married.
But Ella right there, in blue chiffon
it must've been, and waving a wispy
blue scarf and the voice and the
scat singing - do do n dwee dup
was I getting sophisticated! Very
Sophisticated Ladies, Miss Ella
and Miss Sheila from Greenwood.
I have some of those old
round vinyl things, put them on
the record player sometimes
and play a whole world — theirs and mine.

My kids give me remastered CD's
call me if Ella or Nat are on the TV
and sometimes they do that scat singing
my kids, I mean, learned it in jazz choir.
So they put on Unforgettable
and sing to me, full of life, and I —
well let's just say I'm still kicking
and I've still got rhythm and up there
in glory land, I'm sure they do too,
Miss Ella Fitzgerald and Mr Nat King Cole.

Dowry

I owned no record player, age 18,
but did own Harry's "Belafonte"
Brubeck's "Jazz, Red Hot and Cool"
Nat's "After Midnight" (King Cole Trio),
loaned them to a boyfriend, jazz fan,
remember him kindly returning them
to the house on East 14th; something
in the way he said thank you meant
"I won't be seeing you again." He left,
but Nat, Dave and Harry stayed on.
They were long-plays. Age 20
I carried them, (plus a small set
of pink-blossomed dishes),
into my fifty-year marriage.
My only dowry.

Nat King Cole *Mar 17, 1919 - Feb 15, 1965 (45 years old)*
Dave Brubeck *Dec 6, 1920 - Dec 5, 2012 (92 minus a day)*
Harry Belafonte *Mar 1, 1927 - April, 5 2023 (96 years old)*

My *"Spring's Gift"* dishes were a gift from my sister, Jean, for my
16th birthday.

Busker

Violin case splayed on the vast granite floor
he lays himself open, stringy blues tunes
hanging in the air like worn laundry, buffeted
by the breezy self-contained who regularly
board trains with destination in mind. Once
he caught a train into the city, destiny
in mind; never caught another. Prefers,
he says, the trackless freedom of bicycling,
fiddle on his back. Still, in his humdrum
room, a recurring dream: peddling through
lavender fields in the south of France.
Must have seen it on TV.

TV's where he saw the fellow
"who did that pilgrimage thing
somewhere in Spain, walked at least
a hundred miles, hung out in churches
playing fiddle - made it up as he went -
that's freedom - called it playing duets
with buildings - whichever way you turned,
the architecture answered back."

In the familiar architecture of his station,
the busker makes an offering: eye contact (old trick)
and a change-up, a lively reel for the dash to the trains.
In brief suspension of their earnest commute, pilgrims
veer toward the fiddle case, answer back
with a refrain of loose change.

Taping Over

After the symphony we walk Granville Street
so filled with Chopin we can't go straight home.
Street musicians, men from the Andes
with pan pipes, flutes, guitars, hand drums,
serenade us. They shout, whistle, call.
Most of the midnight people stop;
some chuck a loonie in the guitar case.

Then everyone (it seems on cue) is looking up
at a host of seagulls lighted creamy white
by Granville Street. Against a blue-black sky
and a few strong stars, they are tilting
and calling to the men of the Andes.

We buy a tape (they're salesmen too).
We play it over and over not wanting
to let go of the pan pipes or the seagulls.
Now I cannot bring to mind Chopin's concerto.

Bocelli's Bowtie, Pandemic Easter Sunday, 2020

Black bowtie on the immaculate
white shirt of a blind man singing
in an empty cathedral.

Within the ornate immensity
he stands quite still and small.
An organist accompanies,
turning pages; the blind man
has none to turn; his hands rest
at his sides — words and melodies
deep inside, behind his eyes.

He breathes in cathedrals of air
to voice his songs, the heave
of his chest barely visible beneath
his smart Italian three-piece suit.

We who can see listen also to his face —
close-up glimpses of imperfect
teeth, slight flutter of eyelids,
expressive eyebrows — an ordinary man
inside himself singing.

Above the black bow tie, his full lips
caress immaculate syllables into the world:
ave deus, sancta maria,
panis   angelicus,
amazing grace.

Westminster Abbey, Mission BC

*"The unstated theme was the blessedness of gathering and the blessing
of dispersal." - Robert Haas*

The Bach choir was singing
in the abbey church. Small streams
of believers and unbelievers
ascended to the abbey on the hill.

It has always been so, this draw
(in spite of our agnosticism)
to Holy architecture in stone or sound.
We are taken, if only for a time; and time,
I believe, does not thoroughly erase
these moments of arrest.

We were gathered in. We went out,
down the abbey lawns, inside us
a small seed as of mustard,
a smidgen of faith, or love,
or at the very least, hope.

Yesterday

He says he can't play anymore
but yesterday with a little urging
he played — his guitar, old friend,
nestling comfortably into his arms.

He says he can't play like he used to,
fingers not always obedient to
head or heart — but those fingers still
know their way around the frets
drawing music out of that mysterious
storehouse that is the mind or the soul
sending it out to the heart of another.

He says he can't sing anymore
but yesterday he sang. He says
he used to know every Beatles lyric,
then after the stroke, they were gone.
But yesterday he sang Dylan's Ramona,
all the verses. Maybe the singing
will bring back the Beatles too . . .
blackbird singing in the dead of night,
take these broken wings and learn to fly.

"Lean your body forward slightly to support
the guitar against your chest, for the poetry of
the music should resound in your heart."

Andres Segovia

Autumn Leaves

They catch in your hair,
the way words of the song
catch in your throat as they drift
from the stage — the soulful singer
knows the sting. Its name is loss.
A day not seized, a table not spread,
a bed too narrow, love too small,
one never fully let in from the cold.
Or one cherished but taken from you. You long
for autumn leaves to kiss your window,
sun-tanned hands to catch in your hair.

(a response to 'Autumn Leaves' by Kosma and Prebert, sung by Cayla Brookes w. Bill Sample on piano)

Sea, Stone, Moon

Sea, you were silent for the small interior girl.
Your voice did not reach. What she heard
were the water-songs of mountain streams.
How great was your silence as you called her
and all the waters to make their way to you.

Stone, warmed by the sun, large and flat,
perfect for sitting on to think. You held
your tongue, did not interrupt the dreams
of the small interior girl. Still, you sang
the heat of the universe into her body.

Moon, somewhere there's music — and you
were part of that promise, not forgetting to come
in the coldest winter nights. Reach for it, you said
in your quiet way, no matter how high the moon,
reach for the music, small interior girl.

Finding the Horizon Note

"The drone in Indian music is known as the horizon note"
Levertov quoting Henry Cowell

"The health of the eye seems to demand a horizon."
Emerson

Volition downgrades to velleity.
Degrees of disorder prevail. Laws
determine conversion of energy.
Entropy is a word, is a world;
the North side of God is a phrase, a phase -
like the hundred days' wind on a desert in Iran.

The health of the eye
demands horizon. The ear
hears distant pipes, listens
for the drone. A marching band
comes over the dune. The ear
and the eye find their note.

Striped Sea: random thoughts from the shore

The sea's quick-change stripes
sail out from shore in shades of indigo.
By the time they touch the sky,
they're strips of silver.

The language of waves wants
a gift of interpretation. Bach
made a stab at it, a good one.
His indigo fugues, passions, partitas
cut into me like Scripture.

I'm a short piece of sacred
choral music, contrapuntal,
polyphonic, a motet. But how
to sing all the parts? Do you know?

What we are? Perfect
and chaotic and elegant
and ordinary. Elementary
particles, quarks, pieces
in creation's quirkiness.

The striped sea comes
again, again, again. Against
the south wall of the summer
cottage, the drying sunflower
loosens its seeds. They start
falling from the Fibonacci
spirals of their flower-head.

Canyon

"We do not want merely to see beauty ... We want something else which can
 hardly be put into words — to be united with the beauty we see, to pass
 into it, to receive it into ourselves, to bathe in it, to become part of it."
 C. S. Lewis on 'Beauty'

A craving for the Canyon
the Grand one, a place broken open,
not like the crevasse of a glacier
tightening on you, no, an open book,
book of Revelations. Colour of bone
and terra cotta, I imagine it, a place
of descent and staggering ascent,

      where I might fall
silent, tongue arid,

    or talk too much –
tumble of words: skull escarpment
rampart river erode expose uplift !

Sometimes decades will pass without
a step toward what's calling. Sometimes
you wait too long, you get old,
not up for such adventures— though so young,
so nearly non-existent beside the Colorado's
eternal current and the canyon's eons.

My daughter's husband went on an expedition
and I tried to pry from him the canyon's essence,
its gift to him — but he wouldn't say, or couldn't.
Still I'm confident the canyon sang its secrets
into his mandolin. Sometimes for a musician
that's the only way. A composition

is gathering force somewhere inside him.
He has named it "Unconformity"
after a canyon layer which isn't; doesn't
conform, doesn't comply. O musician,
do not wait too long to bring us your song,
wide and noncompliant, canyon-deep.

"If you look deep enough you will see music;
the heart of nature being everywhere music."

Thomas Carlyle

Wild Grasses and Animal Skins

In wind wild grasses bend
and bend me toward their way
of giving even the slightest breeze
permission to play them.

I want to say, world, play me
that way, as pollen-laden winds
play the grasses. Slide your horsehair bow
over the taut catgut, over this little chamber,
my life, with its ungenerous echoes.

Bow and strum me fiercely, though you
break a string. Bamboo flute, drum head,
every stretched skin, every curved enclosure
has its sounds and furies, songs and silences
waiting to be scored. Though I fumble the word,
stumble over it, I will say yes, play me.

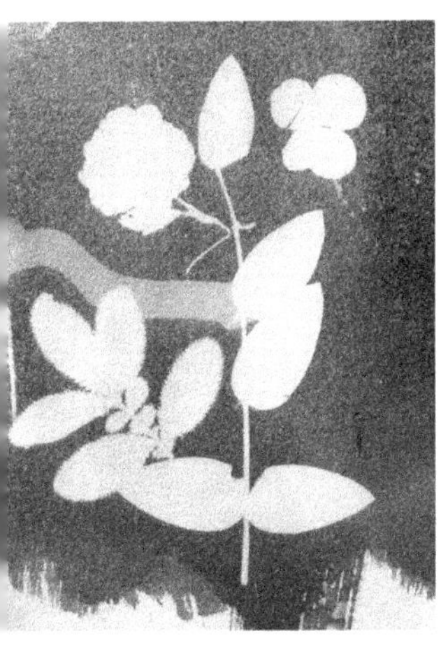

ii

In light
and
colour
and
form

Long Tall Mary

*"Remember that a picture, before being
a battle horse, a nude, an anecdote or whatnot,
is essentially a flat surface covered with colours
assembled in a certain order," said Maurice Denis.*

Thus you could look at a painting
upside down maybe, or sideways.
I choose Denis's 'The Annunciation'
rotated a quarter circle, clockwise,
so the messenger appears
to be causing Mary to levitate
and long, tall Mary floats there
reaching head to toe from wall to wall.

"How can this be?" says Mary.
Still she brings her hands together
as though preparing to dive
into something. The splash
of sunlight coming through the roof
warms the back of Mary's blue gown.
And just over there, Mary's bed.
It's been stood on its head.

The messenger appears
to be rising from a garden,
a lighted place below the open door
which strangely opens upward
like the cellar door of my childhood.

Has the messenger ascended then,
from a world hidden just below the surface
of what we know or allow to be real,
shielding its eyes from the other-
worldliness of our world?

The blinding bright colours: molten yellow,
jewel-red, green, blue — run together,
run over the canvas in one sublime spillage
everything overturned.

(a response to The Annunciation,1912, by Maurice Denis)

The Still Life of Mary Pratt

There is this loveliness in tin-foiled fish
in blood-red currant jelly, in pomegranates
throbbing through bowls of glass
on glass – glimpses of the terrible
beauty Mary sees in surfaces.

Look, look further, further in, further into things.
Look at the painted woman, silent, still
in the see-through light, still as Mary
when she composed herself to paint
the still life stirring in the woman's
severe form. The silent hanging
wedding dresses tell all
the meanings of still:

the leading up to
the coming after
the continuing
nevertheless
furthermore
and yet . . .

[a response to "The Art of Mary Pratt : The Substance of Light"
Vancouver. Art Gallery]

A PSALM

Let all painters praise you, all those who lift their hands
in brave acts of art. Romanticism, say to the people,
"God is and his ideal is love". Realism, say "Truth matters".
Impressionism, impassion the young to see visions,

the old to dream dreams. The expressionist cries out
to you, God, the abstract expressionist and all wild ones –
fauves, dadaists. The surrealist sets us on edge; the cubist
shows us the shape of God whose dimensions cannot be known.

Let the manifold yearnings of the centuries declare you
in this place. Let the Group of Seven praise you
in bold blocks of colour, in leaf patterns and lakes,
in rocks, in jack pines, in cold northern waters.

In this generous second giving, they have offered a country
to its people, what you had made for us of old, and we had
but faintly grasped. Oh that your name might be praised
in light and colour and form from sea to sea. Oh to see.

[a response to "Group of Seven - Art for a Nation", Vancouver Art Gallery]

Where Paintings Hang

Here, by the red bath tub.
As I settle in for a soak
the red tulips
tell me everything
is possible.

Imagination is a buoyant thing.
Tulips can float, foregrounded,
giant and red against purple landscape.

The painter insisted the picture hung
just like that, outside the bus window,
all the way up the North Thompson valley,
dogging her like the moon.

[a response to a painting by Anna Vandas]

Tuscany at the Lab

Vineyards and olive groves,
a defining row of cypress trees
trellised roses by stone houses
with stone steps drawing us in
to that Tuscan way of living, good
bread, good wine and the ever-
present beneficent sun.

Someone rosy and hopeful
has taken time to hang Tuscany
on the walls - in this place of blood
drawn from veins; of urine collected
in plastic vials; of sample kits
given in paper bags to take home
"just read the instructions".

This place of feigned nonchalance,
resignation, embarrassment, anxiety
is a much visited place. We line up
to get in. To wait, To hope.

Bless the rosy someone
who thought we might
want to keep alive
the possibility of a stay
in Tuscany.

Restoration

Mona Lisa, Mona Lisa
release the secret of your lips,
pleasure or shame. Yes, you
in that small frame, having
undergone cleanings,
repairs, restoration,
and a guard set to keep you
safe and immaculate.

Mona Lisa, tell me
about your hunger for touch,
for the salt and grease
of the world's fingers
to restore you.

Why is it I think of you
as I drive down a country road in late summer
toward a feast of fellow poets
while a deer, young and lithe, bounds alongside,
racing me to the salt lick?

*(thinking about restoration after reading Charles Wright's poem on his
attempt to see the fresco cycle "The Legend of the True Cross" in Arezzo.
It was under restoration when he visited.)*

A Daily Advent

Cows amble
toward the call,
(come Bessie, come Boss)
They nudge into stalls.
Mixed feed, silage, dry hay.
Body-warm milk letting down.
The rhythm of milk in the pail.
The darkening barn gathers round.
Then morning's re-milking, release.
The expanse of the fields reclaimed.
New day for farmer and beast, then
come Bessie, come Boss again.

(a response to the painting 'Friesian Cows' by Andrew Macara)

The Bell on his Overalls.

The slim nervous woman behind the camera,
so highly excitable that she normally blurred
all her snapshots, sent a roll of film
to David Spencer Ltd in Vancouver in 1935
where the Kodak Film Department
developed it and kindly sent back
the photo, tinted and enlarged.

The bell on his overalls tells the story:
he was a traveller. The slim nervous woman
would try to keep track of him all her life.
He moved off the farm, no more cows to milk
to the big city where he went to movies,
(not the kind shown in the Baptist church hall).

The big city, where girls wore lipstick
and taught him to dance. A job in television,
then a life not just going to movies,
but making them. Travelling, travelling.
How to keep up to him?
She faithfully wrote newsy letters from the farm:
new tractor; new sprinkler system; new bull
(christened Titus after a book of the bible);
the old workhorses, Duke and Babe still alive.

Every birthday, a card with scriptures
prayerfully chosen, written in her
teacherly hand — her hand less and less
steady as years passed, but the message
always full of longing for her boy to do well,
to be well. She was any mother, every mother,
pinning a little bell to his overalls,
wanting never to lose him.

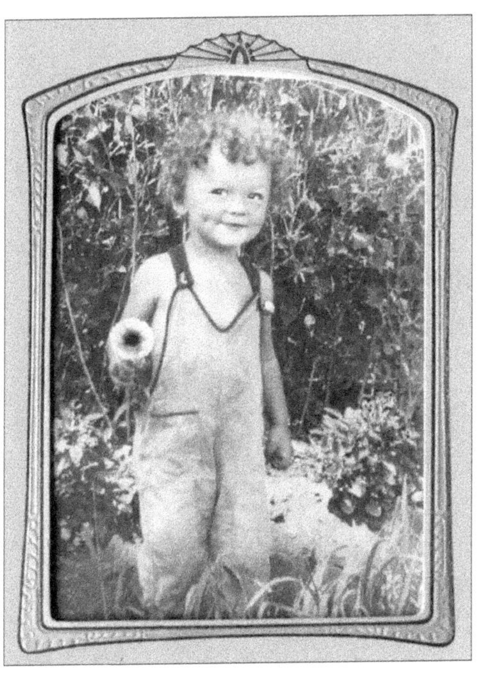

Thomas Merton and the Incoherent Light of the World

"A barn is beautiful if it's a good barn." That's Merton,
seeing the goodness of things. For him, a kind of virtue
was worked into earth's elements at the very start.
God, generous to a fault, fashioned the lens, the retina,
the optic nerve so Tom might revel in the ordinary
incoherent light of creation. Inside the absurdity of ears,
fine hairs, minuscule bones were dreamed up to dispatch
far-fetched messages to Tom's brain for contemplation.

To relish simple goodness in a chemical complexity,
taste buds were made to quicken on contact
with garlic and red wine. The tips of Tom's fingers
could touch in his pocket a broken rosary, a breviary
leather-bound, small icon of virgin and child, dark glasses
in tortoise shell frames to shield Tom's eyes
from the blaze of the incoherent light. All these were left
on Merton's person when he leapt to heaven.

Oh yes, and a Timex watch.
Since the time (or was it un-time?)
when darkness was upon the face of the deep,
since that instant when the incoherent light first flashed,
an incoherently extravagant love has seen fit to sustain
this stained-glass universe. It's Babette's Feast
and Tom urges us to the table. If by ignorance or ennui
we've stayed away, it's time to pull up a chair, hungry
as we are. Latecomers will be seated.

Photo-Graph: "Fifth Avenue from the St. Regis"

A young Alvin Langdon Coburn
crossed the marble-floored lobby
of the beaux-arts St Regis Hotel,
ascended to the desired story
and wrote to us with light.

He funnelled Fifth Avenue's pale emanations
toward the welcome of waiting chemicals.
Fifth Avenue from the St. Regis, circa 1905
made the mysterious oblique leap
onto sensitizing iron salts,
intensifying platinum.

New York, ascendant, misty, mythological,
was caught and kept a hundred years for us
to catch again at Vancouver's gallery
circa 2008. Thus are poems begotten
by the insemination and dissemination of light.

*[a response to Fifth Avenue from the St. Regis, platinum print by Alvin
Langdon Coburn. TruthBeauty: Pictorialism and the Photograph as Art,
1845-1945. Vancouver Art Gallery]*

Tool Box

We see it through the photographer's eye,
foregrounded in the picture, seeming to float,
a once-burdened tool box, heavy in the hand
of the worker, emptied now, contents displayed
in a scatter of wrenches on the work bench,
some rasps, a vise, the many tools of trade, idle.
And surely somewhere just off-stage, a level
and a carpenter's square - otherwise how
such pure geometry: perfect verticals
perfect horizontals - even the sailing masts,
seen through windows, stand, for the moment,
straight up. Pilings, old and sentry-like, continue
upright, reflected in water's mirror. Horizontals
are held level by the practiced picture taker.
The photographer has directed our gaze
from the inside of one old structure past tool box
through the glass of framed windows, to another,
a giant shed still nicely plumb, built, we muse,
maybe with these very tools. Some long-ago
worker/builder/framer/artisan/artist
in a whimsical frame of mind, painted his tool box
turquoise. Now the artist-photographer features it,
seeming to float — but weighty, spilling over
with story in the framed rectangle of this image,
while through the pictured window, the horizon
holds, as level as sea-level can be
on this round revolving planet.

(a response to Elmar Theissen's photograph "Net Loft Tool Box" Steveston, BC

This Poem Wants to be a Camera

Wide shot: colourful chaos, street scene, India.
Slow zoom: woman in light blue cotton, well-aged body.
Close-up: the face, laid bare, arrestingly beautiful.
Dame Judi Dench. Then her English, her voice a cello,
brings us to the brink. Hold the close-up.
Her blue burrowing eyes.

(after seeing The Best Exotic Marigold Hotel)
[Judi Dench has age-related macular degeneration, has to have her
scripts in large print, or read to her.]

Mirror Technology

Is there time within time for time
to replay itself? The whole shebang
captured for playback?

Explorers used mirrors -
a light-handed technology -
to play to a wary native citizenry.
It set some agog, then let go.

Camera, heavy-handed at the birthing bed,
now disallows ephemerality, makes superfluous
those snatched mirror-glimpses of the crowning —
astonishment / wedged / between screams.

Snapshot

Unknown Young Man, Ireland,
jacket photograph, Seamus Heaney's
"District and Circle". Time trickling
or streaming, doesn't come to a full stop.
But the snap of a shot might come closest
to surcease, what we seem to want, warily.

Unknown young man, Ireland
stands outdoors in his three-piece suit
one hand on an 'AGITATOR', forged
in the Philip Pierce & Co. foundry, Wexford.
I don't know Wexford, or what the machine
agitated (possibly turnips) and though I've
seen things, there are many I've missed,
like Ireland and the inside of a foundry.

Unknown young man, Ireland,
an arresting sepia suspension, causes
a small shift and I see there was
a then which is also always, where
an Irishman and a photographer
stopped the onrush and this picture
could be me or you or my father or yours.
Snapshots hoard passing nows, interfere
at times with now's now; now is always
on its way past, becoming then
or forever or never.

(a response to a book jacket photo – Seamus Heaney's District and Circle)

Khromaticos - suited for colour

I'm not from the Island of the Colour Blind.
I've been immersed since birth in blood red,
sky blue, tree green. Colour's not trivial,
not just the skin of a thing. Beets are beets
all the way through. They bleed
into whatever's on your plate.

 Khroma colours my perceptions.
A pansy's face is drinkable purple;
persimmon and papaya taste of colour.
In certain lights your eyes become amber.
Colour is a stairway, an ascending chromatic scale,
to heaven. The sound of red is middle C,
colour of highest energy. (Goethe said so.)

We are khromaticos - suited for colour.
Raw sienna, burnt umber, ochre - the very words
are live wires jolting the painter's pulse. Cerulean blue,
rose madder. Madness to complicate light
for the sake of colour. Could we not have lived
like Bergman and Bogey, perfectly suited
to a black and white Casablanca? Some say
"colour vision evolved when we (monkeys, apes,
humans) switched to diurnal activity; to eating fruit
from flowering plants" - if you find joy in this
survival story of the fittest, any utilitarian comfort
in colour's deconstruction, do think on those things.

Meanwhile a pebble greens under the wave's
wash; your turquoise scarf flashes; the peach
deepens its blush; a single yellow rose opens
my heart; and painters everywhere
throw open their paint boxes.

Cezanne's Chestnuts

He couldn't resist - a row of chestnuts
imploring him to draw.
Our eyes too are drawn with longing
to the siren calligraphy of trees,
their limbs, their slender torsos
pressed against a blue linen sky,
the secret sap rising, falling.

(a response to Cezanne's "Chestnut Trees at the Jas de Bouffan")

Albrecht Durer's Praying Hands

Alas, plaster of Paris praying hands
perched beside bibles - price reduced.
And ah! the pricier porcelain ones
in a classy figurine congregation.
Plastic key-ring praying hands,
luckier, of course, than a rabbit's foot.
Order now, your embroider-by-number
praying hands, available on-line
(embroidery silk in six colours).
Rubber-stamp praying hands, to
endorse best wishes for a speedy
recovery.
           Let us pray - for recovery
of Durer's hands - restored to his body
of work. Albrecht's spirited hands drawing
all the sacred wonders coursing through
his Renaissance mind. Albrecht's hands
in prayer by stylus, by paint brush,
by pear wood and gouge - his effectual,
fervent prayer, availing much.

The Madness of William Blake

*"There is no doubt that this poor man was mad, but there is something
in the madness of this man which interests me more than the sanity of
Lord Byron and Walter Scott" - William Wordsworth.*

God, let the child be, let him run his hoop
along cobblestones, sail his stick-boats in streams.
But no, you had to bless him with visions - angels
and your Self, to carry home to Mama. And that
wasn't the end of it.

                            You, the usually unseen,
inscrutable one, kept a running visual discourse
with the man. Words, though Blake had command
of them, are hardly adequate to translate such verities.
Receptive to all possible conversations, Blake cracked
open his imagination. By ear, eye and all senses,
by all mediums, he produced a searing cinema verité
of the centuries, back to Cain fleeing the world's
first murder scene, back further to a dramatically lit
Ancient of Days. Moving pictures ran multi-screened
through his anointed auteur head - scenes still playing
in a thousand theatres. Who's to say he was not
quite right?

                            Sanity and madness
are not cordoned off; you cross over as you would cross
the equator, not breaking a tape. No marked meridians,
no sign: "you've drifted off course, you sail now
in another hemisphere."

                          Blake sailed on, happily conversing
with long-dead Dante, Milton, Shakespeare. His mortal eye
saw treed angels whistling hallelujahs through unfleshed lips;
his tyger soul roared at devils, giving us pause. Still
his madness is solace to me, giving me leave
to be only as sane as necessary.

Default: Self Portrait

Albrecht Durer, thirteen, took silverpoint
to paper, drawing what he could discern
of himself. Genius already bearing down.
A tender, skillful rendering, first of many
selves he would commit: Durer
at twenty-two, Durer at twenty-six.
Durer, twenty-eight, looking like Christ.

See also Rembrandt: Rembrandt at easel,
Rembrandt as beggar, Rembrandt wide-eyed,
Rembrandt as St. Paul. Likewise Van Gogh:
Vincent with pipe, Vincent with straw hat,
Vincent with pipe *and* straw hat.
Gauguin: self-portrait on tobacco jar,
self-portrait with halo, even
Agony in the Garden: Christ,
looking like Gauguin.

World, body, self. The recurring shove
of the self is from world back to body.
Our eyes are fingertips inquiring
of our skin, the way a blind man
learns a face. We stare at our own
indecipherable stare. Can't catch ourselves
not looking. Even a blurred murky mirror
draws us. We blurt out Gauguin's questions:
Where do we come from? What are we?
Where are we going?

titled untitled

I wrote a poem titled "untitled"
about God -- who's hard to name.
The ancient Hebrews steered clear;
nor would they grave His image.

Someone I know tried to paint God
into a fresco — using Prussian Blue
I think it was The lime ate it up.
GOD disappeared. "What did we tell you?"
chide the ancients, "you can't paint God
into a corner." The inadequacy of symbolic
representation. Tiny three-letter word for
immortal invisible original mover.

Even if you draw it out - gaawwd
like a TV preacher, or a careless curser,
the single syllable doesn't impress.
Webster's traces it back: gott, guth, ghau,
Indo-European, for invoke, call out
ah! . . . mama! papa! god!

Hot Pink

We boxed it up, put the past
in the post and sent it off,
address unknown, into the greening
ether where, it seems, it caught
on the shoulders of an Other —

a hot pink god who was wise
to the hollowness, the darkness
inside our frames, and chose to
bathe our frailty in warmest yellow
light, lining us up for the leap
into deep purple.

*(an abstract response to an abstract painting of many colours
by Carmella Dolmer)*

Across the Universe

*"Love does not consist in gazing at each other, but in looking outward
together in the same direction." Saint Antoine-Exupéry*

In the art gallery, all eyes
are on a singular work of art.
The man I backed into, jockeying
for position in front of Gauguin's
Nude Woman Among the Waves,
accepted my apology in a voice
that was "blackbird singing
in the dead of night".

His eyes said something too; I think
it was here comes the sun. I want
to hold his hand in mine for a time,
hold his face in mind. My thought
is for us to exit together, through
the gift shop, with a view to a tryst
in the gallery's roof top cafe.
All you need is luck for love
to come together right now.

The Engraver

Beginning at the tip of Christ's nose, Mellan pressed
his graver into metal: burin to copper plate. Single-
minded, obsessed, ready, bent on proving
himself able (though unworthy) to carry the face
of Christ to the finish of the spiralling line –
that thin path leading out from the centre.

Mellan had already seen the Moon's centre,
scanned its features through telescope. Pressed
into service by Science, he'd bent to the lens, to line
an artist's moon for learned men. Picture him, single,
nocturnal, capturing the cold solitary face
of the circling body, his assignment proving

his mettle, trying his patience – proving
to himself again, the obsession at the centre
of his character. His exertion showed on his face
as drops of sweat; in weariness he pressed
linen cloth to brow and asked why does God single
me out to be the world's engraver? The line

of grace in his engravings gave answer: a line
of bodily prayer, eye-to-hand prayer, proving
fertile, renewing faith. This all-spending single
soul, errant as any other, grasped the centre
in a spiralling world. Inspired but pressed
by the frustrating finitude of Art, he would face

his own frailty. Dared to recklessness by the Face
of Christ, he received a Word: Grave one line
and only one – Christ's passion pressed
through a pin-hole – pressed wine proving
its truth by taste, like bread. The centre
dot on the page set in motion a single

momentum across Christ's incisive, single
gaze. A fleshed, bone-structured face
for Mellan's inner eye to fathom, centre
on, impart to graced fingers for truest line.
He would draw blood and tears, proving
the rough ruinous beauty of humanity pressed

into the centre of this single
countenance – Christ pressed and pummelled, proving
God. God – a fine line incised on the engraver's face.

*(A sestina in response to Face of Christ on the Sudarium, an engraving
by Claude Mellan - see on - line)*

Worker In Batik

Gloved against dye, salt and soda ash,
she presses parched cotton
down into deep wet yellow,
paints with flourishes of hot wax,
keeps colours, abandons colours.
It's a game of hide and seek.
Dip, dry, wax, and dip again.
Colours collaborate, add up, wax cleaves
leaving needed imperfections – for the beauty of batik
is in the slight seeping through.

Outside the worker's window
a slow subtractive dyeing
is underway: giant maple leaves fall
in remaindered shades of yellow, olive, russet.
Carefully, as though redeeming
some fragile parchment from antiquity
she lifts one leaf from the ground,
places it beside her banners and wonders
"Did some ancient Balinese woman
thus conspire with nature
to dream batik? - or does Fall
never come to Bali?"

One thing she feels in her artist's bones:
this single maple leaf outdoes
her own day's work.
Yellow, olive, russet applied by a colourist
with such attention to detail
that along every vein
there is the needed
bleeding through.

Two Eyes Together

"When I'm drawing one line, I'm creating two spaces."
"One may also be two." Robert Davidson.

Do not let the ravenous
eat even one
        of your eyes.
Two together
deepen your visions
without which we perish.

Were Raven to eat an eye
steal your depth of field
could you draw the knife-edge
that splits the sky; form the line
that doubles space, one
becoming two, an ovum
fertilized, splitting.

Watch both eyes.
Don't let Raven
pick at them; don't let
the ravenous have
even one.

*(a response to Robert Davidson's carving titled "Ravenous" – raven
eating a single eye. "The Abstract Edge", Museum of Anthropology,
UBC)*

Uses of Wood

A light peppering of lichen
settles onto the bench.
Weather, having its way,
engraves its fine striations
into every surface, the slivers
soften and the brighter hues
give way to grey.
Of all the uses wood is put to
it seems this slow silvering
might be the most instructive.

The Weight of Beauty — Exhibition of Fine Furniture

A tree's response to the weight of branching
is a feathering and flowering of the wood's grain.

I had never considered how branching might
put a strain on the trunk, the way a heavy toddler
twists a mother's back into pain. How it might
be a burden undertaken in the natural run
of tree-ness, but demanding and difficult.

I run my hand over the finished walnut table.
It's a visual tumble of waves but smooth
so smooth to the touch from its fine finishing.
The master craftsman tells me how patterns
concentrate around and below the furcations
of limbs. Tree keeps this memory of distress
secret until the cabinetmaker brings it to light.

At the Exhibition of Fine Furniture
I praise the craftsman, his skilled hands,
his eye, his passion. I also praise
the walnut tree for turning its struggle
(can it be called suffering?)
into beauty.

(a response to a walnut table made by Nick Purcell, master craftsman)

A Beautiful Thing . . .

just passed my window:
a buttery-yellow pickup truck,
the old kind, curvy and seductive.
I clapped for it. No-one
was around to laugh at me.

I've admired old pick-ups
painted lipstick red, and once
a surprising baby blue, but never
such a pure creamy yellow —
like butter fresh from the creamery.

Origami

My house-guest, a five-year-old,
folds coloured paper while acquiring
language at an astonishing rate - Japanese
and English. He's teaching me origami and
his mother-tongue. "In Japanese this is . . ."

For breakfast it's nori, rice, vegetables,
sometimes miso soup, nutrition uppermost
in the mind of his Mama. I ponder the well-fed
folds of his child brain, the grid laid down,
neurotransmitters going full tilt,
nicely-folded protein.

He's more. His intense focus will often break
for a smile; and one day he slumped to the ground
sobbing when the ice-cream parlour closed
just as we arrived; and once he took a square
of red origami paper, cut a simple shape
and gave it to me — a heart.

In my own brain-folds, a memory:
another house-guest, old Japanese Pastor
who rose very early the day of his return
to Japan. In secret he folded many colours,
then went softly into my garden to festoon
my one dracaena with paper cranes.

This gladness remained
framed in my kitchen window as summer
folded into fall. Then the rains came,
and the wind, unfolding, scattering.

Fold, fold again; these words want to be
a bright paper bird, but I have no flair
for origami. I cannot find a way
to fold my poem into a pheasant
or a crane, the fledgeling
seems always to falter
though I try to enfold
its palpitating heart
in my palms
gently.

The Perfection of the Maple Tree

Waking early, I move like a nun
toward the eucharist of hours, a day
open to transubstantiation.

Will I be taken up
into the perfection of the maple tree
which stands in continuous praise?

Will sins fall away like dry leaves?

I'm asking why,
or how do you know,
there are error-correcting codes
in the laws of the universe;*

why everything is,
why we are,
so dazzling,
so askew.

NOTES

and ACKNOWLEDGEMENTS

Note that in the second section of the book, **"In light and colour and form,"** the paintings I've responded to can often be found on-line.

Sting - final two lines are from Sting's *"Fields Of Gold"*

Yesterday - final line is from the Beatles' *"Blackbird"*

Canyon - After writing this poem which includes the words, *"the Colorado's eternal current,"* I've read that the Colorado River is in danger of running dry!

Thomas Merton … Incoherent Light is the ordinary light from the sun or a light bulb, which consists mainly of light waves of many different wavelengths or colours. What Light there is of the same wavelengths tends to be out of phase as well. This is in contrast to the coherent light of lasers where the wavelengths are the same and are in phase. Here ends my understanding of coherent and incoherent light.

Across the Universe incorporates phrases from 6 Beatles songs. The poem was written from a prompt: write a poem with the word 'tryst' in it.

07 **The Engraver** I first saw *"Christ's Face on the Sudarium"* while taking a Regent College course in form poetry from Jeanne Murray-Walker. The obsessive and circular nature of this amazing piece of art seemed to call for an obsessive and circular poetry form, the sestina. Apparently the sestina is one of the most complex of the various French forms. It is usually unrhymed, the effect of rhyme being taken over by a fixed pattern of end-words which demands that these end-words in each stanza be the same, though arranged in a different sequence each time. (Google Claude Mellan to ee the engraving)

08 **The Perfection of the Maple Tree** - *"There are error-correcting codes in the laws of the universe"* - a line from a science magazine, re the science of supersymmetry - I don't know what it means.

Piano Speaks Her Mind was previously published in,
Celebrating Poets over 70 (McMaster University, 2010)

The Engraver was previously published in,
Crux (Regent College, 2004)

Default: Self Portrait was previously published in,
Silence, the Breaking of It (Big Tree Publishing, 2014)

Where Paintings Hang was previously published in,
My House Has Many Windows (Big Tree Publishing, 2021)

Worker in Batik was previously published in,
Crux (Regent College, 2002)

Origami was previously published in,
My House Has Many Windows (Big Tree Publishing, 2021)

Several of the poems appearing in this book
have appeared in self-published chapbooks.

THANK YOU

to the following for help in getting this book done.

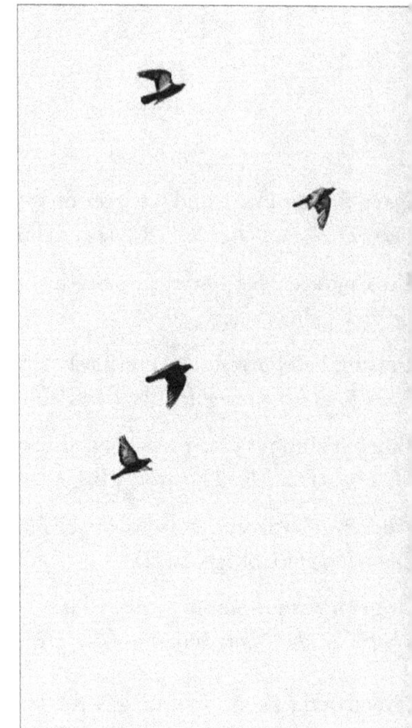

exandrah Pahl

ss Rosen

ane Tucker

z McNally

ark Buchanan

ets, Musicians, Painters,
otographers, artists and
akers of all kinds

Book Design

Discussion & Publishing

Manuscript Reading

Advice & Encouragement

Back Cover Endorsement.

for enriching our lives.